At the Construction Site

Look, a Jackhammer!

By Julia Jaske

A jackhammer can break up
objects inside.

A jackhammer can break up
objects outside.

4

A jackhammer can break
up the ground.

A jackhammer can break
up the sidewalk.

A jackhammer can break
up the road.

A jackhammer can break
up the wall.

A jackhammer can break
up the floor.

A jackhammer can break
up bricks.

A jackhammer can break
up tiles.

A jackhammer can break
up rocks.

A jackhammer can break up
big areas.

A jackhammer can break
up small areas.

Word List

jackhammer   sidewalk   tiles

objects   road   rocks

inside   wall   big

outside   floor   areas

ground   bricks   small

81 Words

A jackhammer can break up objects inside.

A jackhammer can break up objects outside.

A jackhammer can break up the ground.

A jackhammer can break up the sidewalk.

A jackhammer can break up the road.

A jackhammer can break up the wall.

A jackhammer can break up the floor.

A jackhammer can break up bricks.

A jackhammer can break up tiles.

A jackhammer can break up rocks.

A jackhammer can break up big areas.

A jackhammer can break up small areas.

CHERRY BLOSSOM PRESS

Published in the United States of America by Cherry Lake Publishing Group
Ann Arbor, Michigan
www.cherrylakepublishing.com

Photo Credits: © mipan/Shutterstock, cover, 1, 14; © jiangdi/Shutterstock, back cover; © SGr/Shutterstock, 2;
© Oleg Kopyov/Shutterstock, 3; © deadandliving/istock, 4; © jrphoto6/istock, 5; © Sergii_Petruk/Shutterstock, 6;
© Miljan Zivkovic/Shutterstock, 7; © Simon Kovacic/Shutterstock, 8; © KHANZEL/Shutterstock, 9; © vchal/
Shutterstock, 10; © Prapat Aowsakorn/Shutterstock, 11; © Sophie James/Shutterstock, 12; © chomplearn/
Shutterstock, 13

Cherry Blossom Press is an imprint of Cherry Lake Publishing Group.

Library of Congress Cataloging-in-Publication Data

Names: Jaske, Julia, author.
Title: Look, a jackhammer! / by Julia Jaske.
Description: Ann Arbor, Michigan : Cherry Lake Publishing, [2021] | Series:
    At the construction site
Identifiers: LCCN 2021007847 (print) | LCCN 2021007848 (ebook) | ISBN
    9781534188235 (paperback) | ISBN 9781534189638 (pdf) | ISBN
    9781534191037 (ebook)
Subjects: LCSH: Jackhammers–Juvenile literature. | Wrecking–Juvenile
    literature.
Classification: LCC TJ1305 .J37 2021 (print) | LCC TJ1305 (ebook) | DDC
    621.9/52–dc23
LC record available at https://lccn.loc.gov/2021007847
LC ebook record available at https://lccn.loc.gov/2021007848

Printed in the United States of America
Corporate Graphics